Wake Wake Wake

Also by Valerie Nieman

Poetry Chapbooks

How We Live
Slipping Out of Old Eve

Short Fiction

Fidelities

Novels

Survivors
Neena Gathering

Wake Wake Wake

Valerie Nieman

Press 53
Winston-Salem, North Carolina

Press 53
PO Box 30314
Winston-Salem, NC 27130

First Edition

Cover design by Elisa Barger
Cover art by William Brian Hibbard

Lisel Mueller's quote on the back cover was taken from
her introduction to *Daily Rhythms: Three Women Poets*,
a special chapbook issue of *Sing Heavenly Muse!*
Valerie Nieman's *Slipping Out of Old Eve* was one of
three chapbooks selected by Ms. Mueller and printed in
Issue No. 15, 1988.

Cover art, "Kayli," by William Brian Hibbard,
used with permission of the artist.

Printed in the United States of America

ISBN 0-9772283-5-5

Acknowledgments

The author thanks so many Gentle Readers who had sharp teeth when the poems demanded it. Thank you to the Dayton Hudson Foundation and *Sing Heavenly Muse!*, Kentucky Foundation for Women, West Virginia Commission on the Arts, State Street Press, Central Piedmont Regional Artists Hub Program, *Phoebe,* and especially the National Endowment for the Arts, for their support. Thank you to Tim Russell for years of Zen insights, to Sarah Lindsay and Fred Chappell, who guided the manuscript in its final stages, and to Kevin Watson and Sheryl Monks for their love and labor on this book. And most of all, my thanks and love to Jack, for always believing.

Grateful acknowledgment is made to the publications where these poems first appeared:

"A Moment's Peace," anthologized in *And Now the Magpie*, Mountain State Press; "Changing the Landscape," and "Night Alone," *The Dickinsonian;* "Covet," and "All the Trimmings," *Phoebe;* "Duration," *The News & Observer*, Raleigh, NC; "Eager," *The Pedestal Magazine;* "The End of Capitalism," Farming anthology, Pudding House Press; "First Generation," *Tar River Poetry;* "Farm Wife," "First Generation," "Hanging Up Clothes," "The Increase of the Earth," and "A Moment's Peace," chapbook *Slipping Out of Old Eve* in *Sing Heavenly Muse!, 1988;* "Formalities," *The Sow's Ear Poetry Review;* "Hanging Up Clothes," *The Greenfield Review;* "How We Live," "This Place," "Elementals," "Hanging Up Clothes," "Mirabilia," "Nuptial Dances in Fire Time: Suite," and "Above Dunkard Mill Run," chapbook, *How We Live*, State Street Press; "Indulgences," *5 AM;* "Mirabilia," *New Letters;* "Pennies a Day," *Kakalak 2006 Anthology of Carolina Poets;* "Persephone in Suburbia," *Poetry;* "Pissing in the Woods," *Fresh Ground;* "Pissing in the Woods," "Above Dunkard Mill Run," and "How We Live," anthologized in *Wild Sweet Notes: Fifty Years of West Virginia Poetry, 1950-1999*, Publishers Place, Inc.; "Police at the Scene," *West Branch;* "Thunder," *REDiViDER*

For Brad and Hunter and Sarah
ad astra

Contents

III Stir Up, as Passions, or Evoke, as an Echo

Wake Wake Wake

Wake Wake Wake

I

What Has Passed

Call

The boys have learned to whistle.
They ride their bicycles
up and down Elam, straight
from Fernwood to Fortune
and back, their piercing
notes signalling the others:
sunburned, scrape-kneed, eyes
narrowed as they scout the neighborhood.

How did they learn? Not from fathers,
absent or exhausted. Indian tales
are as out of fashion as feathers,
leathercraft, Fenimore Cooper,
yet they ride like Comanche,
pumping their bikes
and then standing on the pedals,
arms sunward, note answering single note.

Even dead center of the city, after all,
the cicadas crawl out of their skins
and leave them, small lamps, on the maple trunks.
Possums gorge on ungathered pears,
and the sharp-shinned hawk,
fashioned for woods-work, banks
between power lines and porch
to take a sparrow in mid-whistle.

Plotline, with reader

The summer my father had a heart attack
we got a color TV,
and every Saturday morning watched Wile E. Coyote
engineer doom with rockets, anvils, boulders,
nitroglycerine like his pills nested under cotton
in a vial in the "Eggs" compartment –
two a day for years, the pills dissolving
under his tongue as he sat in the recliner
watching the Browns hammer the Steelers.

This is where the story forks:
you expect that the watcher was watched,
his shallow breaths measured against
the blue light from the tube,
chair arms slowly denting under his fists
at a bad play 300 miles away,
his advice unheeded, curses unheard.
And you would have his heart shatter,
body slump under a surf of inveigled shouts.

But the plot takes another path,
my father learning the pain came not from clenched
arteries but from a tear in cartilage, a crack in his chest.
A new doctor tossed the nitroglycerine
in the trash, no crash, no boom,
no resolution, my father plowing on day by day
until he retires to sit in the recliner
watching football, and my mother sits on the couch
watching him, the explosion always just over the horizon.

Pennies a Day

Fragments of soap migrate
from shower to sink. I can't throw them away,
but at least never pressed such slivers
and skipping-stones into a motley cake,

useful through the first shower,
when the parsimonious bar shatters,
and the fragments are gathered—again?
and pressed, the glycerins

holding the whole together
like noodles or rice to stretch
the meat across another meal.
We always had enough,

I don't recall hunger—
though a child's only a greedyguts
squall for more, more—but I do remember
the sound of a fingernail on steel,

my aunt loathe to loose a quarter
for a Chore Boy to scour away the scorch,
so she hunched over sinkwater gone flat of suds
and scratched. Scratch scratch,

the sound of a fork on a melamine plate,
pushing gristly bits around to find
a little meat, sopping bread in thin juice.
My father's fork. My mother's.

First Generation

You spade the kitchen garden
each spring, turning the fine,
dark dirt loose from the years.
Gladiolus you planted for your dead wife
sprout again, sharpened green,
opening smaller and smaller
yellow faces that wag red tongues.

You mutter peasant German
going backward in the row,
planting potatoes
under a dark moon,
planting peas, planting cabbage
by the signs.
Does the seed know
those stick-shaped words
you never taught me?

At night you walk the rooms
of an unwarmed house,
your steps too short
for a man as tall as you have been.
You write letters in pencil
on blue-lined paper, careful English
dancing in German shoes.
The table where you work is ring-marked:
for years it held plants on saucers, cuttings.

When she died, these died also.
After a time, you stacked the pots
in the cellar.

You write me letters
telling of the cold, of summers
that are shorter and shorter,
and I am south, feeling the sun
earlier and later,
feeling here that I have failed my blood.

Your eyes have become paler blue,
and I would want to say
the color of March sky,
thin lines on paper,
or lilac petals, faded.
They measure out
this distance between us,
the rivers and the days,
and mark out the unseasonable shadows
that sharpen along the road home.

Elementals

Ridge farm, early spring:
I nose along the wet
belly of the land,
the hummocked fields,
dead grass furrowed
by voles and frost.

Here: A waft of skunk,
maybe the urine
of a fox,
or flesh leaking
from the nibbled arc
of a fungus.

A sycamore limb cracks under foot
to the length of a hiking staff.
Brown decay clings to my palm,
fragrant as the spotted
flanks of a trout
hooked from cold water.

A pond hangs halfway up
the slope, suspended in a net
of willow and poplar,
tarnished silver
held up to a particular sky
between ridge and field.

Water lies quiet in this pocket
as a forgotten dime, while everywhere

in else-slanted earth it runs,
footing through clay
caves domed by recent frost.

A skin of ice is pinned
across the pond,
but here and there
dendrites of open water
spark, live cells
the breeze makes flicker.

Dark drifts of pods
like those cast, egg-full, on beaches
testify to locust trees
that bloomed last summer.
In each silken womb curl
eleven little pigs the color of old blood,
their umbilici brown and white.

Deer, surprised, part
like guilty lovers.
One flees down the slope,
sensible winter coat
beginning to blush spring-russet.
The other, a buck,
climbs toward the ridge
with newly bare head erect
so that phantom antlers
do not tangle in grapevine.

Branches of red maple say their name
over and over.
The ruby buds are alternate,
three and three,
at the end a perfection of nine.
Saint Acer, readying
a burst of saffron prayers.

Paper-wasps build words
into their nests,
each cud of digested tree carried,
spat out and palpated;
added rows mimic the accumulation
of an oyster shell,
exhausted waves on a beach,
rings of muscle
in a gray eye's iris.

They are faithful to a Gothic
obligation to enclose space,
to build apse upon apse,
and choirs
where the February sun chants.

The nest is fragile as rice paper,
yet, orphaned to the wind,
it has survived.
I play its pan-pipe hollows
more by breathing in
than out.

Farm Wife

You can tell a country woman
by her feet.

At midsummer, see the lines
at the backs of her bare heels
like cracks parched in clay,
channels abandoned in streambeds
by water that ran in April
and lipped itself back
to its source come May.

Her feet sink into the garden soil
as deep as stones.

Translate this ogham-script,
these lines incised
on worn granite flesh,
a text on the good wife who
rises early to skim the cream
from last night's milking,
and who works late,
ironing muslin sheets,
her fisted hand passing and passing
through the steam;
oh she is better far
than rubies.

By harvest the blood of her weariness
drips from her broken feet
and sows itself amidst the ripened corn.

Pissing in the Woods

Need that crouches behind a screen
of young hemlock
that pulse
heavy
as monthly blood in the belly.

I perch
boots apart
settling heavily
into last fall's duff
but release will not
come
old shames
old fears
air on buttocks and the intimate grass.

Lean into a young tree
friend and prop
recognize
black cherry from glossy bark
that rambling weed as
New England aster
poison oak
(of course)
and beginning its climb
convolvulus.

My stream does not arc
a proud horse's neck
of intentionality
nor fall straight.

Schooled muscles
refuse
clench
relax
the spray veers
runs down my leg
twisting a path
to earth
wetting leaves
and soil
fragrance on its way
to ammonia.

I leave a marker
like the doe
by the pond
that pauses
urinates
moves on
restless
for the buck that follows
tastes her need.

Expedition

She walked until the river split into streams,
streams to creeks, creeks to runs
and the last run like a dark thread
drawing her into the land itself,
into a closed wound.

She had lenses for looking up and counting
the stars and lenses for looking down
and counting springtails in the blackened leaves
and some that were only mirrors.

She penciled entries on the pale
machine-drawn lines of her journal—
the first morning bird (indigo bunting),
the way alder leaves were chewed and tattered.
At first she ignored broken beer bottles,
plastic jugs impaled on branches,
until they disappeared.
"One tire in the water," she wrote,
then left the rest of the page blank.
"A girl's hair ribbon, brown with algae,"
and she walked upstream, the ribbon
waving behind her, a single meager thread
useless in the great maze of the land.

Once people came past her camp,
sang hymns
washed in the blood of
the sweet by and
nearer My God

and she thought they were angels
until a voice broke and she cursed
them and their victim.

The moon came night after night,
round then horned.
When there were clouds then the sky
was a perfect swollen gray,
like the inside of a ball of wool.

A hunter stood at twilight on a ridge,
listening to distant hounds.
He tended a fire, stirring it with a stripped
and broken limb. Sparks whirled up.
He might have worn a red plaid coat,
a letterman's jacket with demons
or dragons, something extinct,
might have worn leaves for leggings
and braided vines.
She watched his movements
until he became a figure
marked with a burnt stick
on the wall of the sky,
jumped into life by a fire's emaciating light.
She turned to her own small flame.
Her arousal spiraled into the night air
and extinguishment.

The land shut around her.
She tried to climb the bluffs

but found the way too vertical,
treacherous with abrupt springs,
spalled stone and clay.
The water no longer seemed to flow past
but knot and tangle, a black net
heaving in the rapids, at the narrows.

She fished with a line twisted
from her hair and knotted
to a hawthorn hook, caught minnows
and ate them quivering whole, their silver eyes
seeing the way down her throat,
scales clinging to her fingers
like the light of the absent moon.

In the fall came a flood. Her books,
pages long sealed with mold and fungus,
went like unearthed coffins
on the brown tide.

She ate lethargic ants
and grubs with useless fat-man's legs,
peeled the bark from cherry trees
and chewed the green lining, like the frayed
lining of her coat.
She killed a belling hound lost to the hunter,
and fallen as she had
to the bent snare of the land.
She seared its flesh over a fire lit

with alder leaves and berry canes
and fed with the litter that accumulates
on the upstream side of a leaning snag.

The trickle of water was a gash in the frozen land.
She wore the dog's hide on her blackened feet
and the dog's head on her own,
fangs permanently bared.
She watched ice creep out from the banks,
knit itself together the way
bones heal, swords cross,
random marks of the unlettered
are sent tongueless to the future.

Slovan to Burgettstown

Wasp nests sway just above the semis
running this two-lane cutoff to Weirton,
twisting past closed pig-processing
plants, video stores and Pentecostal temples,
houses with their feet to the highway,
corrugated panels turning back the slush,
all the women foreshortened, men
broken under their pompadours,

the back doors of the VFW, Eagles, Slovak Club,
K of C, Moose and Legion,
garbage cans filled with last night's kielbasa,
the up and down into Weirton,
steam plumes streaming into clouds
that lop the red and white smokestacks,
limp flag twisted around its staff
above parked cars, street-corner sons of hoopies

tethered to wire mills and tool-and-die shops,
tows of coal three abreast digging deep
on the bend, the Ohio sheer mercury, the tugs
making no headway toward Pittsburgh,
houses crabbing up the hills from the river,
street above street bent around the armature
of the Appalachians, house next to house,
not a stride between them. Strike
this place with a stick
and all hell would break loose.

Police at the Scene

One too few for pallbearing,
they watch the river
but concentrate on their feet—
polished black oxfords dangerously
willing to the slope—
don't see the coal train drawing
a line on the opposite bank.

> She came to the bridge wearing only
> her husband's topcoat,
> which she took off, folded,
> and boxed in a square of sidewalk.
> Who would have thought
> that in January
> her calmed mind would shatter
> through the ice,
> the slim rod of her body
> making small emphasis in the decorous white?

The police find her troublesome,
are afraid her body
will be snared by branches
and bleach bottles taken in the freeze,
or that like a hornet blundered into a house
she'll bump that imposed white sky
all the way to the Lock and Dam,
losing skin, losing features,
rounding to anonymity.

> But she waltzes feet-first,
> limpid as this river

never is:
her family appreciates her now
for this calm, this silence,
this unaided tranquility,
not knowing that she's broken all confinement,
her body's five pints
dissolving into the river,
sooner, warmer,
an ocean.

Much water goes by while they sleep.

The police get cold, go home,
ask what's for dinner but don't hear the answer.

Above Dunkard Mill Run

Every farmhouse rides
at anchor in a phosphorescent
harbor of sodium vapor lights;
every cargoed barn
waits for the tide-turn.

Our roofline is long, square
as an ark, and we rise
prow-high against the swells,
sailing into dark fields
on this late warm wind.
Smoke drives from our chimney,
      North,
      North, baying
like geese
high and invisible, white
reaching toward the white
that holds off—
building like a typhoon
over open ocean.

Deep inside, we
feel the lift
and settle, the creak
of timbers, wind-
bent, borne up
as though righteous.

How We Live

Bay leaf and pepper, mushrooms,
garlic, sometimes juniper berries,
vinegar and onion: I have my own
familiarity with the doe
you shot in our third field;
my hands trim
the yellow rinds of fat, wake
the spark lying quiet
in this dense red grove.
Sometimes,
despite your scrupulousness,
I find a fine brown hair,
zoned with the colors
of concealment like fur from the cat's back
or the way my hair turns white.

Some people cannot abide wild
meat, the resinous aroma,
the color
like knife-openings
in the palms of their hands,
blood loamy as old
wine and thick, unmingled with water.
To eat and live:
like breathing in and out,
and acknowledged or not
there is always
some spiral toward coldness.

Still, those of us who eat
have a duty to know—to hunker down
and smell fresh droppings gleaming
like berries on the path,
hear the snort of the lead doe
warning into flight
a band of yearlings,
in uncut fields
to walk our way into the beds of deer,
rounded as the stopping-place
of boulders, where a moraine
knuckles under inexorable glacier.

Trompe l'Oeil

The storm to the north
is still as an averted face,
lightning so flat and frequent
along the motionless cheek
that it seems a trick
of the eye,
a warning of glaucoma,
some blinding awaitment.

South, white thunderheads
climb each other's shoulders
from the drowning blue
of the horizon. A planet candles
in a narrow space, soon occluded:
the *Farmer's Almanac*
could not now or ever
recall its name.

The fireflies
rise and rise. This early
they lift from damp short grass
and curing hay;
later they will move purposefully
across the black,
blinking like electrons
vaulting a cloud chamber.

I am surrounded
by faint clickings, unexplained,
a dry dark crackling like a Geiger counter
held to the thorium-soaked white nets
that incandesce in a barn lantern.
It would be pleasant,
reassuring, to believe
that with each lumination,

each firefly signal,
came this tiny sound:
a lamp turned on
in an upstairs bedroom
of a farmhouse with asphalt shingles,
the switch-chain clicking back
into its place
one brass bead at a time.

Hanging Up Clothes

Out in the last fine rain,
the light red in the west,
after the storm.
A delight for the eye
and tomorrow.

A deer comes from the wood line
and stands deep in daisies,
watching.
My white-flag work
does not frighten her.
The red light glows
in her summer coat.

The light is red.
The deer grazes.
I move from line to line.

Damage

She sees I've broken
three toes, or four. Bare
feet recall wet grass, warm soil—
and splinter, and sting,
root, rock, sill.

She hangs up her dress:
the green vault
of the closet breathes out
her perfume, the pressed-cotton
of his white shirts,
and from her cloth coat
with its mink collar flattening,
camphor.

My mother bends,
releases the locks of her garters
and her stockings slip.
Her feet, free of spike heels,
ease flat on the worn floor,
but the red toes press together,
raw as new kittens
scrambling after a tit.

Bunion, hammer toe, callus:
hidden flesh aches,
born wide and loose
as aberrant children
who in darkness are bent
with appliances, straps,

torsion devices, their splayed
happiness gripped into civility.

Past inheritance
of tendon and bone:
broken and broken
to one shape, her feet
becoming my own.

Duration

The Swingline Speed Stapler 3
was surplused out of the front office
not long before the whole enterprise went belly-up.
What a piece of work this is!
A Chrysler building, an Eames chair (but humble)
polished chrome, matte steel,
its rising curves lifted from a Hudson,
from the front a sphinx of good order,
and each part—
from the cross-hatched footplate
to the cracked rubber palm-pad
incised with three decorative lines—
my God look what attention to detail
and proud of it,
patent numbers here, and here,
this work of Long Island City New York:
decades later the spring
is still full of the old zip.

A simple machine, to take a bit of wire
and bend it back on itself, papers secured at a thwack,
or a bulletin board tacked into place
with the easy release of the staple arm
from a metal catch (made in U.S.A., patented),
a more permanent fix
than Post-Its.
My father passed it along
when I headed to college—a reliable tool

like the clipboard and mechanical pencil
he used on the shop floor
ages and states ago. A move here, a move there—
I could have stapled maps
of the Eastern United States together
to trace the routes, the cities where things are made
and traded, where I stick
for a time, and then (unfastened) lift away.

Persephone in Suburbia

If I stop
stirring for one moment
this delicate sauce will curdle
and my hand, allowed to
rest, will curl into the shape
of a shrunken leaf

> bare twigs of the single
> chokecherry tree gleam like ruby
> pressed into narrow life
> in deep basalt

If the sound of children pauses,
the bassoon voice
that underlies their treble
will become plain
and they will freeze
until I race the lengthening shadow
around the cul-de-sac,
touching their blue temples

> the days are still warm
> but at four in the afternoon I find dew
> beaded in that wild pocket
> between lawn and woods

If for one moment I fail
to pray this house
square on its lot,
chant the laundered curtains
just so, intone perfection,
the lawn will crack apart

along seams marked
by the lime-spreader's wheels
and there will be no recovery

> I know now that the interior
> of a pomegranate is a hive,
> berries vibrating
> their muted life,
> waxy membranes impressed with hexagons
> as in all things
> which move, or are still,
> shape and function are preserved

One by one by one
I nibble the red bees.

Wake Wake Wake

II

A Watch by Night

This Place

The bearded stranger chants old names:
      Davis, Bennett, Hoy, DeGroot,
families twice removed, forgotten like second cousins,
their farms parceled
and the names they set here
tailing off like the farm road to Davys Run,
gone to a depression in the running hay.

      There were two ponds, one above the other ...
      Only the one now, sulphurous, shrunken,
      the higher pond drained down to marsh.

      And the long field we planted in corn ...
      Hay grows now, and around the sickle curve
      at the back, a stand of dogbane.

      The others were in wheat, my father
      drove the horses that pulled the thresher ...

      At the point of woods was a persimmon tree,
      look for the fruit after frost ...

What this stranger knows with his feet
and the reach of his arms,
what I can't recognize or is no longer there—
even the flats where hogs
rooted up a Confederate belt buckle
(so he says, and I want to believe)
are overgrown with box elder, sassafras,
crabapple, ash, trees stem-green

as grass, so quickly
the land throws itself into forest.

> In the meadow I find
> coal and limestone, fire slag.
> *That was where we shod the horses ...*
> The Cutlip places sifts into its foundation
> and my dogs go in and out the windows.
> *I lived in that house,*
> *by the flats, below the fields.*

We hold to it
like the mole whose pale hands
knew the ground better than either of us
until it was turned out, broken,
belly up under the porch
where the post begins to settle,
its hands palm-up,
narrow and thumbless
like the warding hands of saints.

Changing the Landscape: Suite

1 Moving Trees

They would lay across my life
heavy as two legs,
seven feet of sheared
spruce implying the eventual

burden. The Christmas trees
planted southeast-
northwest of the house
are the poles of a dangerous magnet,

      Salavi, the spruce tree,
raises his arms like a man
who has nothing to hide
and I don't believe him, instead

I'm moving out of that charged
diagonal, taking up the trees
before their branches
blacken at seventy feet.

      The roots are knotted
in the ground and I pry like a house-
breaker; the woven roots snap
and cry righteousness.

Each tree weighs as much as a body;
the yellow rope sings
as the spruce goes up the hill
on the tumpline of my outrage.

Spruce trees stand now
with young cedar
along the north line,
bearing lightning.

2 *In Springtime*

We are allotted
a hundred springs, at best,
one hundred times the first open earth,
one hundred times the rue anemone on the hillside,
one hundred times for the bell-bird to begin,

when there are a hundred irritations
in a day, a hundred chores in a week,
and the body's chores, the washing of hair,
clipping of nails, the decades-long
washing out of the body
in menstrual blood.

This is the 39th time
I've seen the grass flame green,
but the split does not heal.
Like the fracturing of a cliff face
by frost, the legend of trees
detonated by Alaskan cold,

the break in mid-winter
unhealed, unhealed.
I look for you to come home,
come up out of the woods like a deer, shy and forward.
I watch until I see only
the plum tree white against unopened forest.

3 People Say, Rage, Rage

I check each dark basement
room each night,
not for security—
if I found someone
what could I do?—
but the reason without a tongue
is that you might be there,
a prodigal kneeling
in the ashes by the woodstove,
or a traitor
who has hung himself
from the great beam
he once balanced on his shoulder.

4 Taking by Fire

The fire has been laid
since morning,
a pyramid of cherry, locust,
oak, maple,
poplar, a pithy bolt
of black walnut, my gift,
on top.
The straw
tent pitched inside
breathes fire
into the wood.

When I was a child,
the neighbor's barn went up,
a summer's yield of hay roaring,
and the bugling terror
of Holsteins locked
in their stanchions.
The sparks flew so far
that the Randolph firemen
relinquished the barn
to the fire
and came across the field
to spray water on our roof.

And when you and I were first
together, coming home
from Buffalo late,
the world not yet turned
into the dawn,
we followed a glow in the sky
for miles,
drawn to it by the requirement
of roads, that glow
a conflagration,
the red barn at Clark's Corners
losing its color between
white fire and the uneasy night.

Tonight, enclosed by field,
sky, stream,
I stand close to another
four-walled flame, throw on these
dry things I hold:
some words,
cedar for spiritual strength,
sage for wisdom,

I let go all the rest.

5 Reclaiming the I

Small words around which
a life settles—you, we, us—
being taken out,

the I shapes a raked
landscape, smooth sand circling stones
in pools of silence,

mountain and ocean
in stone and pool, juniper
for tall mountain spruce,

eddies of force as
strong as the binding power
inside the atom.

The End of Capitalism

I am celebrating today.
I've put a white shirt on.
        "In Integrum," Timothy Russell

The ownership of a hunk of ground
is the nearest heaven I've imagined.
11.17 acres, house lot, three hayfields
going to dogbane and thistles,
a child of my body,
as though I'd opened my legs
and the meadows flowed out:
They were the first thing I let go,
handing them over to Charlie and his tractor
and his men hoisting the bales.
I walk fields that are greening again,
mine yet on the courthouse books,
but the other night,
Charlie came and trimmed the fence lines,
swaying like a lover in a waltz.
The garden went this spring:
I gave it back to grass and clover
that had long asserted squatter's rights.
Goodbye, goodbye. My neck eased,
my feet quit hurting. Now
the house must go, too, all its corners,
the hidden boards scribed with my father's blessings
and ex-husband's imprecations, goodbye, goodbye.
Soon all I'll ask is a robe
and a bowl and a space of pavement,
then only a body, but that, too, will be
relinquished.

Night Alone

The trees, remembering
that they are sky,
go back to it,

sky emptying
snow among the branches,
the branches lifting

up their dark selves,
the burned-work
of sun and air,

the living cinder,
until sky and tree
are the same,

are night,
and my shuttle
soul lies down.

A Moment's Peace

Not that she's not the finest
woman a man could have,
you understand, as steady
as the chestnut beams
that hold up this house,
heart solid like good oak.
But for months I've been
waiting to slip away,
waiting on a time her heartbeat
and breath didn't fill all the house
and hold my life to my ribs.
A moment's peace
so that like a scarred old tomcat
I could slip away
and die without grief.

A miner's life goes on
as long as he feels
the shift of the earth around him,
knows the strain of slate
against roof bolts,
the dead air, the black damp
and the gas. I've felt my death
waiting for me before—once
I was buried to my waist
in a roof fall, one time
pinned against the face—
but death closed its red eyes and retreated

when the rescue teams came.
It's been here
waiting a long time, now,
in the useless hollows of my lungs:
black lung, they say, and emphysema,
the word like air hissing out
a punctured chest.
But Norma, this time,
shakes her fist in the face of death.
She stands over me
like a cat with one kitten,
like a slender pine tree
rooting together the broken face of a cliff.

I hear the mailman's pickup
grinding up the road;
he's a friend, unseen,
a friend like any man whose cap light
shines on you in a close place,
promising relief.
The mailman doesn't realize
that the minute Norma takes to run down
and get the letters
is the day's freedom for me,
the only time she leaves
this house. Other people come and go,
she stays, her breaths drawing deep
and urging my own shallow

sucking at the bottled oxygen,
the labor of thirty dark years
waged all over again
in my tunneled lungs.
Norma and I, we are flesh of each other's flesh
and closer than ribs, even
the stacked bones of the spine.

✒

She's back, pushing into the squeal
of the screen door,
shuffling the letters
and the printed circulars
that I read cover to cover,
prices compared, the soft colors
of women's sweaters that I never
before had the want or time to consider.
"Bills?" I ask,
the oxygen vibrating in my nostrils.
"Some. And there's a letter
here for Mr. Sam"—her nose wrinkles—
"Harry must've mixed the bundles."
"Oh," I say, but can't
summon the breath for more.

✒

"It's government, got to be
important," she says. "And no mail

again 'til Tuesday."
I see her gauging the distance
to the old man's house,
five minutes at most.
"I suppose I ought to run it down to him."
She looks at me, propped
in the white of my hospital bed,
and I try not to whisper
go, go.
"I'll just be a minute,"
and she leans over and kisses my chin.

The screen door squalls
and bounces shut,
but she stands outside.
I can feel her, waiting, listening.
I breathe in and, struggling, out.
Her shoes crunch on the gravel,
down the driveway,
past the mailbox like a guarded gate
and onto the road.

I've been portioning out
my breath, waiting.
The house is quiet, absolutely

quiet; it eases like a church
when the parishioners have gone
and the flowers have been taken
from the altar.
The window glass shivers,
feeling that she's gone, the linoleum
sighs with a strain relieved,
the water pipes sweat.
I see a bird's shadow move across
the window glass.
I see the shadows of the trees
on the floor
like the branches of a thicket,
green shade against the July sun,
a retreating place.
     I see my breath move across
the light, swirling
the bits of dust
and then they swim undisturbed.

Covet

Mr. Cates, he's dead.
His widow creeps to the car
invisibly through the breezeway.
He likewise left behind
a thirty-foot aluminum ladder
that hangs on the back of the shed.

My gutters are clogged,
and I've wanted to ask her
for the ladder, but thought
I might break open some old wound.
I might as well go over
and fire up that brick barbecue
he built, a hearth
you could spit a pig on,
side grill, wood storage,
warming box with its own tiny door,
all this ziggurating
up to the chimney.

The late Mr. Cates
laid bricks and blocks,
painted the shutters,
built a carport,
drove the posts
for a split-rail fence,
weatherstripped the doors
and windows,
and put a gaslight out by the street.
All I want is the ladder.

When It's Over

I turn everything off twice,
each faucet, every switch,
my fingers lingering on the porcelain.

In the middle of each room
I catalog the dangers
quieted: TV and stereo unplugged.

I screw down the taps behind
the washing machine; I point
at the computer, off off off, off off off.

Chain the back door, turn the key
in the front door, left, right, locked,
rattle the knob, the brass tongue caught in its catch.

And then in the cool darkness
I stand, hands in my pockets.
The house hums under its breath, a dynamo,

electricity circling
in the walls, magnetic fields
arcing wide, away, and back.

Eager

I know what's going on down there:
A week and a day after burying my dog
in the iris bed, the rains have come back,
the blue sky relents,
and the clay heap over her body darkens, eases,
flowing as fluids seek their level,
entrances become exits.

Once I watched a black snake
carried back into earth.
It had thrashed itself to death
in netting meant to save my strawberries;
I cut its body free and tossed it,
a good four feet of lank muscle,
into the ravine that cut down to Buffalo Creek.
I came across it later,
then day by day knelt to watch this circus
of mortality, the burying beetles,
black and red, undermining the soil
to drag it down, while ants carried flecks of flesh away,
and maggots tunneled. The scaled skin held longer
than expected, then the vault of ribs showed,
a frame left as a busy village dispersed.

I agree with my mother: no embalming,
no formaldehyde, cotton batting
to plump out the sagging skin, no rouge

or dye or hair pomade, or (worst)
thread drawn from nipple to nipple
to tent the breasts.
Her mother, a tough creature
like a hazelnut, round and impervious, who had survived
lumber camps, diphtheria,
TB patients spitting around her feet,
five childbeds—no mystery in all this
making and unmaking—took her tenderest daughter
along to the mortuary. That girl, my mother,
clutched at skirts as she saw her father
naked, tubes carrying out his failed blood,
carrying in the embalmer's craft.

Better to burn.
Better the silence, sky, vulture beaks.
Best to let the earth do as it does.

                        *

Oh, the words offered and the nectarine
and then the kiss—so easy to fall in love
for the third time, the fourth, how many other leaps,
knowing there's nothing under my feet,
nothing all the way down. Still, I always levitate,
until absence leaves me to ponder mortal
leadenness and I plunge.
Knowing what was going on
down there, I chose never to watch

as the body of love uncoiled,
it being dangerous to stare fixedly
at any dazzling thing.

The dirt is soft to the pressure of my foot,
giving ground where her head would be,
pointing west, the whole grave
held down by the trunk of an apple tree
split to death by ice. She was the last gift
of a marriage that not long after dissolved.
It's easy to eulogize
a dog, her loyalty less complicated,
happy obedience in moves
from country to village to city;
now in Carolina soil
she comes apart.

Lint

The lawn gathers mortality in July—
today, a shrew killed
in the midst of its own small predations,
long nose still
as a bluebottle investigates.
Also bird feathers,
the molt strewing them like the burst
of a dark pillow,
most being starling, from the flocks
that rustle in the bull-bay
and flare away at a slammed door.
Cigarette butts.
A cup from Jersey Mike's.
A cicada shell,
the insect flown from its creeping life.
A single squib
from a string of firecrackers,
green tube patterned
with white flowers.
I tap it against my palm
expecting gunpowder,
but what comes out is pale, dry,
the cracklings of this season's drought,
dust from a lawn that might
erupt on a hot evening,
each blade going off, pop pop pop pop.

Wake Wake Wake

III

Stir Up, as Passions, or Evoke, as an Echo

All the Trimmings

In the Chinese restaurant
he's opening one cookie
after another, empty,
each an aperture
without an image,
chamber awaiting the bullet,
the explosion
spiraling up the vena cava
from the cardiologist's glove,
quack line-reader
finding fate lopped short
at the foot of thumb hill
in the palm's moist meadow,
relentless squaring
of the field under the machine,
a shrieking fawn
in the haymaker's arms,
his boots locating one front hoof
then the other.

Nuptial Dances in Fire Time: Suite

1 Woodcutting

Lovers abandoned to fading wilderness,
without instinct to plait bowers,
we pile branches green at the cut,
furred ropes of *Rhus*—
snake-twined, venomous—
grapevine stripped from poplar and cherry.

We trace spirals
of May-dance, out of season:
The sweat on your neck
        last sating nectar of summer,
        and yellow-jackets swarm.
Confetti of maple leaves
        and locust-wood shavings
        saffron and red on your wrist.
Blue-green of wild garlic
        sharp with spring
        among the crashing leaves.

Spilled oil, scorched metal,
trees cut cross-grain,
planed hot and smooth.
A voice raw in the back of the throat,
raw as the shout of one
who has danced too long.

        Nuptial round dances,
        and all fall down.

        Like these sectioned trees,
        lie back in my arms.

2 *Fire Season*

From the south,
from Braxton County,
Boone County, Mingo County, Logan County,

a heavy, stinging air
with the vanilla of certain pipe tobaccos
drapes thick as summer fog.

The distance grays, as if filled
to the soft horizon with these sudden
whirling-down shales of hornbeam.

3 *Montani Semper Liberi*

The hills are not his.
Grandfather sold the hidden blackness
of the land, and her womb shudders.
Great-grandfather sold the trees,
gone and replaced, gone and replaced,
wearily virgin.

> "Behold, thou art fair, my love;
> behold, thou art fair;
> thou hast doves' eyes."

The lover of fire
comes in to the land, to the green
hills his teachers
taught him to sing.
He lights a cigarette, savors
the draw of smoke
and how the ember delicately
takes the paper in its teeth
to make more of itself.
He shares as with a friend, passing
it in cupped hand to the tinder
edge of a leaf.

> "Behold, thou art fair, my beloved,
> yea, pleasant: also our bed is green."

He sits on a mossy bank,
nervous hands now loose on his knees.
When smolder flares
the lover of fire leans forward,
his tongue touches the roof of his mouth
and the secret name;
his blue eyes cloud with outlawed beauty.

Gorgeous flame,
licking scorch, flaring
can-can ruffles of red and black,
teasing ribbons, gauds,
veils that lift
to the tree-tops and whorishly fall,
revealing all right to the bones.

> "The beams of our house are cedar,
> and our rafters of fir."

His bride whirls,
smiles as her limber spine
      snaps.
      She bears, bloodlessly roaring,
      a child of smoke.

      At the wail of the siren,
      he drives to the fire hall
      for his shovel and his rake.

Mirabilia

Reflections on Leslie Fiedler's Freaks

It made me think on God, she said,
and the Lord Jesus;
the bell pepper
halved by the knife revealed
another perfect fruit inside.

I wondered why she didn't ponder
instead the image of Mary, womb heavy
with evident man, immanent God,
or any mother who infuses her
most personal blood
into the body of an intimate stranger.

Vegetable prodigies are shown around
to family, friends:
potatoes with famous noses and chins,
squash fused into male genitalia,
Siamesed strawberries.
Pictures of some appear
in the local newspaper,
so that we, accustomed to the world
as it must be,
accept also the burden of the strange
that is.

◢

The man whose brother nested
head-first in his stomach

gazed into the camera
and the ordinary world,
tenderly grasping his brother's
frail wrists above velveteen sleeves.
For the audience, he dressed the other as a woman,
although he knew the parasite
was the same gender as he,
the autosite, the host.
The One-and-a-Half had a name
he never revealed
for this other, this body plunging into his own.

In the 17th century, Lazarus Colloredo
and his pendant brother
(named for John the Baptist)
were christened together,
mirrored foreheads crossed with holy water,
each saved from a subsequent hell,
priests and cardinals
more willing to admit a vacant soul to heaven
than attest that behind closed
eyes some thought might not
coil forever inward.

The wet legless carcass
was a puppy—black fur soft as a mole's,
a naked belly, a brush of whiskers.
I turned it over with the spade,

wondering how my affectionate dog
could have shaken the life from a form
not so unlike her own.
The scalp was pulled forward
over a tender skull
the color and texture of a peeled
Santa Rosa plum:
innocent, innocent, innocent.

Once they opened
a stillborn boy's augmented skull
to find five brothers
parenthetically
bending silent heads together.

The Increase of the Earth

God help me I didnt want to wear my hair
knotted at the back of my head like something
put there to hang me up by,
just work me out wring me out like
a dishrag, hang me up to dry
wrinkled

no, I wanted my hair to be as wide as the fan
moving the hot August air away from my face in church,
spread like the tail of a mockingbird
when it goes to light on a branch,
wide as a field of young corn
needing hoed
and longer than a river

that night Jamie laid me down my hair
stretched from my ears to Atlanta.

A bodys gonna eat a peck a dirt,
anyways

dirt draws itself up out of the places where men spat,
from the feathers of wild birds shot over fields
growed up too thick to find them out,
from slops of dishwater thrown,
bones of mice and legs of cows

that the dogs carry about after the slaughtering,
all into the red clay

I scoop up the dirt in a silver teaspoon
that I found by the side of the road, the handle bent,
the bowl of it tarnish-black,
dirts pressed out from rock like sugar from cane,
I recollect a teacher saying, and when its done
the mountains lie down flat

I think theres enough of things
falling down into the dirt
that the mountains dont have to worry,
the bones will build up of themselves

I put the spoon in my mouth
and chew the dirt like it was gristle to my teeth.

◢

I remember that night with Jamie
not so well as the night before,
like the night fore the electric come

lines was strung on the locust poles
and bulbs hanging from the ceiling,
round and white and empty, ready for the juice,
berries hanging for the sun to fill them up

now to remember the night before better than the night
itself—and with the sweating
and him shuddering over me,

all just quick as a shooting star that leaves a streak
of more-dark when its gone
it was just a minute or two
and the waiting was so long after,
it dont frame itself the way the night before did,
the darkness while we waited, not quite sure
how the light would look

not knowing it would make the shadows darker
where they hunkered in the loose fronts of coveralls
and creept amongst the chairlegs.

Im out of season, swelling up now in the cold weather
like buds in a false spring,
and fearing I might be headed to the bitter
and the blight

this baby grows out of my blood
Ive stood enough times in the cornfield
after rain, heard the sound of roots drinking up
hissing it was so fast

in school I looked through a microscope once
at dirt—roots thinner than the finest thread
running everwhere, embroidering floss
untwisted, amongst the grains of sand,
little animals, worms,
thats soil, the teacher said, not dirt
its alive
I could have told her that

I feel like a cannibal sometimes
open my mouth and its filled with blood

I worked in the canning factory
this summer gone by

a body had to sit inside in that
heat and stink to eat lunch,
outside the wasps swarmed that thick
around the waste and piles of skins

tomatoes coming down the belt all day
I reached to take one off and when I touched it
a green worm came ramping up
big as my thumb
and my stomach jumped
I vomited right then and there on the belt,
and it carried that off
with the tomatoes

after that I worked near the door
and ever morning my stomach
went ramping up
I kneeled on the dirt,
head down, me and the wasps.

The midwife holds my baby up
she aint marked, she says, after a long silent

time of looking for the kind of strangeness
shes seen before.
no extra twisted fingers, or brown marks tattooed
in shape of bones or teeth or horns,
a rat that mightve gnawed
or a storm that frighted

my baby comes from between my legs red
with the clay, red and slick as the road after a rain.
Ive birthed a child of mud
out of a womb of dust

dont slap her
my daughterll breathe in the clay
and never stop of earth-eating.

Thunder

The dog is nervous:
Porch rearranged, chairs
pulled in from the screens,
all the angles askew

as rain peens on the metal
awning and I muse how much
I enjoy rain at night
on a tin roof, but that's

a borrowed liking, a friend's
red roof where rain hammers
and snow groans
to the edge and over,

her farmhouse (grayer, gaunter)
bent around my childhood
stairs. I fell straight down in the dark
to the yellow kitchen:

uprush of light and heat,
my bare feet
lipping the top step, balance
forward, body tumbling

to my mother at the white stove
turning on the red O
of her mouth

as the dog,
chained to his peaked house,
raised his muzzle around a howl.

A Gift of *Collected Sonnets*
"I know my mind and I have made my choice."
—Edna St. Vincent Millay

Oh, we can waltz this waltz, brother, elide,
allude, misdirect the sight from the raw
sear of your friend's flesh to mine. You saw
the kiss, his mouth grazing my throat, and tried
with Millay to undo what I will do,
reciting wisdom, but I page to pain,
refuse your Zen for outcries, spells, refrains
of desire and restless nights. Thank you
for this tender gift, this worn book, mill dust
stippling the bent back pages, each thumbed
by your millwright's hands, red stained and numbed,
when in your surreptitious hammock, rust
of Weirton Steel compounding on your dreams,
you seethed advice for later pouring out,
expecting the urgent call to weld shut
broken lines, with bare hands embrace live steam.

Adam and Eve as Fire and Water

The first thing he had to teach her was how to break
a line. She had a tongue like every silver thing
(minnow, brook, icicle he named,
ermine and salmon) but lacked structure.

Here, he said, snapping his fingers,
here, and her thought cracked
with a puff of steam, leaving sharp white ends.
She licked the sap from parted words.

> Water covers fire.
> Fire makes water flee.
> They were stones whirled at the end
> of a cord, flying apart, falling together.

He carried her from place to place
in the garden. She rotated in his hands
like a piece of fruit,
then slid through his fingers,

re-formed at his feet, a mirror pool,
raised herself into a wave, enveloped him.
For a moment he guttered,
pulling down around his hot center,

then he found the oxygen in her simple form,
broke the bonds, fed.

Exc. Location, Pvt. Ent.

You can have the right ventricle—
it's plush, though smaller perhaps
than you'd hoped.

Never mind the thumps
and howls from the next unit;
she's been there for years,

a long-term tenant, impossible to dislodge.
The whispers, ignore them,
a murmur of no importance

like the one that blew out
your cousin's sweet-16 heart—
unfortunate, with property so dear.

The rooms upstairs are small
and busy with ghosts, lots of coming
and going. You'll get accustomed.

Really, this place has never been occupied.
A little smoke damage, minor.
You could do a lot here—

A nice rug.
Put up some curtains.
That sort of thing women do.

Fishing the New River

Surely you said
a maple leaf, I've caught

a maple leaf,
but I heard maple seed:

I called back
"samara," winged fruit,

like us, pressed
together at the seams,

belly to belly,
spinning to earth

on the green angels
of our pasts.

Hibernation

You've been sucking your paw
long enough to prove the legend:
Milk seeps from the split of your toes,
juice stored up a hundred years ago
when you rolled in the cotton grass,
in the cub-fat rough and tumble
accumulation of days.

Your hair and skin are slick,
mossy where the slobber runs;
your claws are soft.
The deeper the cold, the richer
your savor of honey and grubs,
dewberries, upstream salmon,
a woman. You remember her.

Then forget. Since winter set in,
you've learned to take it all
out of yourself. Flesh melts;
leaching bones tent up a pelt
famine-red and lusterless
as if toasted
before someone's comfort-fire.

You suck your left paw,
then your right,
it's all night these days,
all darkness developing
at the back of your eyes.
Down on the bay,
the water groans:
Ice in? Ice out?

Advent, Turtle

One foot forward,
old ebenezer, red-eyed, beaked,
claws digging into wet leaves—then,
suspicious of something looming,

the foot pulled slowly back,
hiss of exhalation, lungs folded,
limbs bent to safety inside the strongbox.

You should be chin-deep in cold mud, waiting it out—
so what's meant by this late moving,
this creak of cartilage like the pine tops

swayed by a wind that doesn't reach down here?
I lift you up, and set you back beside the path
heading the same way, lacking better indication,
hearing that we have all fallen short.

Indulgences

All that'll save me from the fiery furnace
is the small servanthood
of replacing the toilet paper roll
in the office restroom.

Or maybe handing a buck
to the shave-headed boy at K-mart,
caught mute at the difference
between his desire and his crumpled means.

Alms given without tax deduction
might put a thumb on the scales of justice,
but I believe that what'll free me
is moving turtles to the side of the road:

Soles scorched on hell's fresh asphalt,
lungs filled with sulphur,
I'll be caught up, unburdened
by something given sometime I don't recall.

Formalities

Easier not to begin,
to cross my ankles
and arrange my hands
into the elegant form
of the reader—
first position,
hand on the spine,
spread, one finger
poised at the edge
of the page—
so that when
the woman turns
with her tract,
alert to this person
sitting behind her,
I am a study
of book,
black shirt,
a face on which
nothing makes an impression.

The hand must be
positioned here, the left leg
raised so, for entry
to be maximized.
This same old
carnal sutra,

carved in flesh,
never translated
properly in stone
or text or moving
pictures, but the fear
of desire keeps setting it down,
damp hands parting
sex books, always the same
Euclidean limits
on how the body folds,
(these slippery proofs),
enumerating positions
like times tables
to be overcome.

My father sings
the wrong hymn
all the way through:
tone deaf, to him
these chords are mere
vibration, phrasing
that might just as well
be German or Swedish.
After the chorus,
my mother's hand
lifts the page,
stabs at the number.

He holds the book,
prays, lifts up
the green ribbon
that marks the liturgy's return.
He runs his finger
along the words,
showing her, as always,
where it begins.

Green Heart

(for Jack)

It was exactly November, when
oak leaves even must relent
to the migration,
skating south to ground,
burrowing to soil, to root, rootlet,
finally tree heart pumping vertically.

All the browns of every ground
a puzzle that only resolves
when you don't focus too closely,
the way a path is best walked
not by looking down,
but by looking out

as we did then,
new, old, afraid to look too much to each other,
to allow that green heart
wild in the woods, until the echo
of our feet on a bridge crossing no water
made us stop, embrace, let go.

Claim

Imagine there is a desert island
just offshore—land shadows reach across
while the sea is still bright,
so it's named Leila, which is night.

Watched, the isolate
becomes the object of desire, invites
the open hand—what was ignored, inviolate
acquires a history—

a landing party
drags tents and cots atop the rock.
Here, they say, our generations herded flocks,
in this cave, it's said, Phoenicians—

enough.

Imagine there is a small green island
in the ring of your right eye.
When we walk through woods the slant
light catches its shape.

We clasp hands so close
there is no space allowed
for the quaver of sorrows,
the clang of history—

and on an island, unwatched,
off Morocco,
a family herds goats to the spring,
singing.

Valerie Nieman is the author of two novels, a collection of short stories and two chapbooks of poetry. Her poems and short stories have been widely published in journals such as *Poetry, The Kenyon Review, 5 A.M.*, and *West Branch*, as well as several anthologies. Her awards include a poetry fellowship from the National Endowment for the Arts, the 1998 and 2002 Elizabeth Simpson Smith prizes in fiction, and the Greg Grummer Prize in poetry. A 1978 graduate of West Virginia University, she received an MFA in creative writing at Queens University of Charlotte. A longtime newspaper reporter and editor, she is now an assistant professor of English and journalism at NC A&T State University.

William Brian Hibbard is a professional painter and sculptor, and is actively a part of the growing art scene in Greensboro, NC. Born and raised in South Carolina, he received a Bachelor of Fine Arts, with a concentration in painting, from Winthrop University. Hibbard's artwork can often be seen in North Carolina's prestigious homes and public spaces.

In 2000, Hibbard moved to Greensboro from Santa Fe, NM, and began working as an apprentice to a nationally recognized sculptor during the day while painting on nights and weekends. His first public art project was in 2001 when he designed 40 panels for Greensboro's *Millennium Gate,* and worked as well on the fabrication and installation. By 2003, Hibbard completed a public art mural in Black Mountain, NC, paving the way for his own business.

The year 2004 started with an article in *Southern Living* and a one-man show "How I See It" at the Greensboro Artist League, featuring over fifty new paintings. Hibbard completed two murals for Holy Trinity Episcopal Church and Natty

Greene's Restaurant by the end of that year. In 2005, he installed three gates and two bronze plaques for Greensboro's new baseball stadium. Carol McCreedy wrote a wonderful article on his paintings entitled, "Renaissance Man," in *Triad Living* during the summer of 2005.

In the spring of 2006, Hibbard installed a 9' x 22' mural that overlooks the new Center City park in the heart of downtown Greensboro. William Brian Hibbard's work can be seen at one of his numerous solo exhibitions or at his studio at Lyndon Street Artworks in downtown Greensboro.

Cover Designer

Elisa Barger earned her Associate of Arts degree from Peace College, and her Bachelor of Science degree in Commercial (Graphic) Design from Appalachian State University. She says, "My life has been inspired by a grand passion for art. My life has always included a love of drawing, painting, music, poetry and theater."

During Elisa's twenty-year career she has worked for a nationally known magazine publisher, an advertising and marketing agency, a newspaper and a printing company. She has designed a variety of media including packaging for Planters Lifesavers, logos for Pepsi Direct and Wake Medical, and promotional material for Wachovia and Wake Forest University. She has also designed CD covers and promotional materials for nationally known musicians. Elisa is now self-employed as ElisaDesigns (www.elisadesigns.com).